LIVES
AND
TIMES

Emmeline Pankhurst

Margaret Hudson

Heinemann
LIBRARY

First published in Great Britain by Heinemann Library
Halley Court, Jordan Hill, Oxford OX2 8EJ,
a division of Reed Educational and Professional Publishing Ltd.

OXFORD FLORENCE PRAGUE MADRID ATHENS
MELBOURNE AUCKLAND KUALA LUMPUR SINGAPORE TOKYO
IBADAN NAIROBI KAMPALA JOHANNESBURG GABORONE
PORTSMOUTH NH (USA) CHICAGO MEXICO CITY SAO PAULO

Designed by Ken Vail Graphic Design, Cambridge
Illustrations by Christa Hook (Linden Artists)
Printed and bound in Italy by L.E.G.O.

01 00 99 98 97
10 9 8 7 6 5 4 3 2 1

ISBN 0 431 02474 X

Some words are shown in bold, **like this**.
You can find out what they mean by looking
in the glossary. The glossary also helps you
say difficult words.

British Library Cataloguing in Publication Data

Hudson, Margaret
Emmeline Pankhurst - (Lives & times)
1. Pankhurst, Emmeline, 1858–1928 - Juvenile literature
2. Suffragists - Great Britain - Biography - Juvenile literature
I. Title
324.6'23'092

Acknowledgements
The Publishers would like to thank the following for permission to reproduce photographs:
Barnaby's Picture Library, p.23; Hulton Deutsch, p.16; Mary Evans Picture Library, pp. 17, 18, 19, 20,
21; Museum of London, p.22;

Cover photograph: Mary Evans Picture Library

Our thanks to Betty Root for her comments in the preparation of this book.

Every effort has been made to contact copyright holders of any material reproduced in this book.
Any omissions will be rectified in subsequent printings if notice is given to the Publisher.

Contents

The first part of this book tells you the story of
Emmeline Pankhurst.
The second part tells you how we can find out
about her life.

Early life

Emmeline Pankhurst was born in Manchester in 1858, more than 130 years ago. When she was twelve, she went to a meeting about who could **vote** in **elections**. At that time only men could vote.

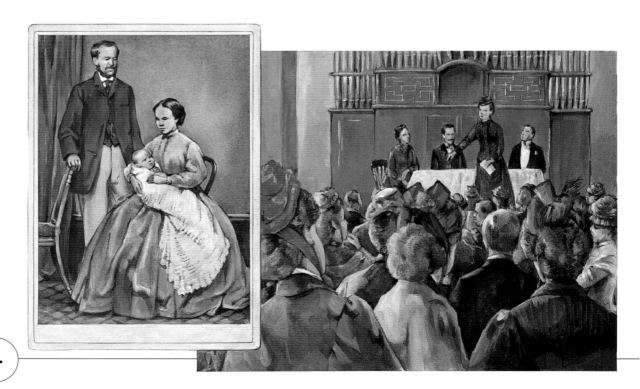

In 1879, Emmeline married Dr Richard Pankhurst. He died in 1898. After this, Emmeline spent a lot of her time trying to to change things so women could vote too.

Suffragettes

In 1903, Emmeline and some other women got together in a group. They all wanted women to be allowed to **vote**, and wanted people to notice their ideas.

They held meetings. They also interrupted other meetings, even **Parliament**. Some of them, like Emmeline, were arrested for doing this. Newspapers called them **'suffragettes'**.

Prison

After 1909, the **suffragettes** began to break the **law** to get people to notice their ideas. First they broke shop windows all over the country. Some of them became more violent.

They set fire to letter-boxes and even
MPs' homes. Many suffragettes were
arrested. In prison, they refused to eat,
so food was forced down their throats.

Too violent?

In 1913, the **suffragettes marched** to Buckingham Palace. They wanted the king to support them. There were fights with the police. Emmeline and many other suffragettes were arrested.

Many people turned against the suffragettes, even people who wanted women to be allowed to **vote**. They felt that the suffragettes were too violent.

The First World War

In 1914, a war broke out. Lots of men became soldiers and went away to fight. Who would do their jobs and make weapons for the war? Now the **government** wanted women to go to work.

The **suffragettes** helped to get women to
do the work. Women drove buses and
worked in factories. They showed that
they were as good as men.

Last years

When the war ended in 1918, the **government** made new **laws.** They allowed women aged 30 and over to **vote** for the first time. Some even became **MPs**.

Emmeline tried to become an MP in 1927, but did not get enough votes to win. She died in 1928. That year the government made a new law. Now all women over 21 could vote, the same as men.

Photographs

There are many ways for us to find out about Emmeline and the **suffragettes**.

People took a lot of photographs of suffragette meetings, **marches** and arrests. This photo shows Emmeline being arrested in May 1914.

Writings

There were many stories about the **suffragettes** in the newspapers, and we can still read them today. Suffragettes often did things which would get them noticed by the papers. This helped to spread their ideas.

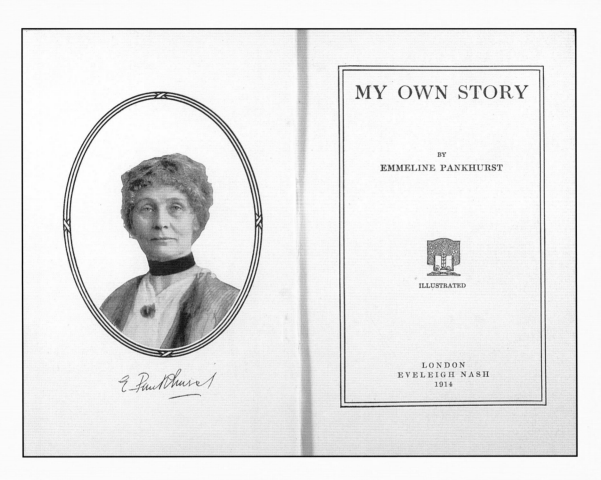

The suffragettes also produced their own newspapers. Some of them even wrote books. This is Emmeline's book about her life, *My Own Story*.

Posters

Not everyone agreed about letting women **vote**. Posters, like this one, were on the side of the **suffragettes**.

TREATMENT OF POLITICAL PRISONERS UNDER A LIBERAL GOVERNMENT.

Some posters were against the suffragettes. The postcard you can see here makes fun of them.

Badges and statues

Here are some badges which Emmeline
Pankhurst and the **suffragettes** wore.
You can still see them in museums.

This is a statue of Emmeline. You can visit this statue in London. It shows that people think she was important.

Glossary

This glossary explains difficult words, and helps you to say words which may be hard to say.

election when people choose someone to speak for them in **Parliament.** You say *ee-LEK-shun*

government the people in **Parliament** who run the country and make the **laws**. You say *GUV-ern-munt*

law rule that everyone in the country has to obey

march a group of people walking together to show their support for something

MP stands for Member of **Parliament**. Someone many people have **voted** for. He or she goes to Parliament to help run the country

Parliament group of people who run the country. Each person in the Parliament is **voted** in. You say *PARL-eea-munt*

suffragette woman who fought for the right of women to **vote** in **elections**. You say *suff-ra-jet*

vote choose one person in an **election**

Index